Stewed Balloons an‹

CW00469761

D. J. Pullar

<u>ACKNOWLEDGMENTS</u>
To my Dad

Thanks to everyone mentioned within this book for their contributions to my memories of these events. The names of none of the characters described have been changed so as not to protect their identities, as I felt everyone should be held accountable for their actions and feel embarrassed or proud where appropriate.

Thanks also to my son, Stephen, for his help in the composition of the original copy of this story.

I would also like to thank everyone who helped me with the writing of this short story, especially to Alyson Rice who, although came very close to slapping me during this long, arduous but, enjoyable process, managed to restrain herself and we got through it together.

This short story, tells the tale of my family, headed by Mum, Margaret, and Dad, Ron, who both worked tirelessly and devotedly for their house, family and of one fortnight in particular.

PREFACE

To put you in the picture, our house was in a cosy, sleepy residential estate. To us children at this time the house seemed huge, although, looking back on it now it was average for that time. Downstairs it had the usual kitchen and bathroom. Off the kitchen stood the dining-room come living-room. At the front of the house was the good room (front room) with Mum and Dad's bedroom across the hallway. The last room downstairs was the back bedroom which was used for overnight guests, although once, during the golf Open at Carnoustie, my Mum did bed and breakfast and rented it out to a man called Peter Sellars, (no not that one, a salesman, not the Pink Panther). Upstairs were two bedrooms. Being the oldest, I had a room to myself and Andrew and Douglas shared the larger one, which was fine with me as that was the room that housed the water tanks. This meant that every time the toilet was flushed, you could hear the gurgling of the tanks refilling and it seemed to make a constant low, hissing noise accompanied with a drip from the ill-fitting ball cock. You would think that my brothers having to live with this continual noise would bother me but I had my own room so I couldn't care less. It was their problem. Besides which, Mum assured them they would get used to it, which after a week or so they did. It made this noise for months until Dad relented to Mums orping and got round to fixing it.

The house sat within its own grounds, surrounded by four small lawns. The bane of my Dad's life! Not so much that it was hard work or that he didn't like them, it was more that he liked to make sure they were always kept tidy, but that took a lot of time, time he would have preferred to have spent with his family and not maintaining the lawns. There was also apple and plum trees to the rear of the house. At the foot of the garden stood the double garage, bursting at the seams with everything imaginable . . . apart from cars, that is. They were parked on the drive or the street, to save having to open the big gates! There was also a small unpainted shed in which Mum had a large commercial hairdryer, which was kept as a memento after she sold her hairdressing salon. Nowadays, it stood in this old, unpainted shed and was only ever used for my Gran (Nanny) who would be left out there with a coffee and a magazine whilst her perm set and her hair dried and possibly the occasional friend that managed to twist Mum's arm. This, it seemed, was the only time that Nanny ever sat still. Any other time you would find her cooking, cleaning, hoovering or busying herself with anything she thought she could do that would help Mum.

The final member of the household was Whisky, our West highland terrier. She went everywhere with us......Well that's where we lived.

CHAPTER 1

The three of us were on the side lawn playing shooty in against the hedge. Dad was cutting the back lawn while Mum was at the kitchen sink watching us with the football.

Dad came around and said, "If you want to play football, go up to the park."

We all sighed as the park was at least three whole minutes' walk away, so we went in to the living room to watch the football results. By this time Mum was in the front room adjusting the clock. She seemed to be having trouble getting it to sit just how she wanted. She was a slim woman, with long, golden hair and a fair complexion. Nimble, fit and quite attractive . . . well, for her age anyway! She could not get the clock, which had a large, round, pale brown face with plastic rays radiating from it resembling the sunshine, to sit exactly as she wanted with its two foot pendulum swinging back and forth.

At that moment, Dad sauntered in followed by the dog to see what she was up to. Dad, was an early middle-aged man, with a heavily Bryl-creamed Bobby Charlton-style comb over which stood to attention when the wind blew in the right direction. A strong aroma of Old Spice and cigarette smoke announced his impending entrance to the room.

"What are you up to, darling?" he inquired, "And can I be of any assistance?"

"You leave it alone!" Mum snapped. "I don't have the right screws for this. I will have to go to the shops to get them. Don't you touch it! We all know you couldn't even put a nail in a dumpling!"

So with a raise of his eyebrows and a shake of his head he watched her depart for the shops, then lighting another cigarette, wandered off. After a short while his nose got the better of him and he decided to go back in and have another look at the clock.

Peace and quiet for the three of us watching the football in the other room was interrupted by the sound of hammering coming from the front room. We all looked at each other inquisitively and, one by one, decided to go through to see what the noise was.

Being the oldest, I went first, pursued by Andrew, who had thick, blond hair and finally, Douglas, who was the youngest with a mop of curly, dark hair following at the rear.

The source of the noise quickly became apparent, when it was revealed that Dad had stupidly hammered two large, rusty nails into the wall on which he had then hung the clock.

"You were told to leave that alone Dad!" I commented.

"Yes, well, it's done now and working fine! I just need to touch the pendulum to make it start," was the snarled response. And with that he gave the pendulum a slight nudge. It immediately sprung to life, swinging to and fro. Then with an almighty crash, it fell from the wall and smashed on the floor, followed by the two rusty nails which bounced along the carpet and came to rest at Dad's feet. With this, he shrugged his shoulders and made a swift exit from the room, leaving us dumbfounded and staring in aghast at the broken pendulum on the floor.

A few moments later, Dad returned to the room, Super Glue in hand, and inquired. "When's your Mother due back?"

"Should be about an hour," was the answer.

He quickly set about gluing the piece of the pendulum back on to the clock. As he was doing this, Douglas informed him that the packet said that it would take two hours to dry and reminded him that Mum would be back well before this. Unperturbed, he put the mended clock on top of the Calor gas heater so the glue would set quicker before disappearing out of the room once more, heading to the back door with a cigarette in hand. On his way through the kitchen, he stopped at the oven, opened the door to examine the beef cooking, as was his propensity. On closing the door of the cooker, he tweaked the thermostat to full heat as he liked his roast very well done and continued out the back door.

Back in the front room, we were now examining more closely the masterpiece of repair work left behind by Dad. Douglas commented that he didn't think it was a good idea, and Andrew added Dad had done it so it must be a bad idea.

The three of us then decided to return to the living-room to continue watching the football. By now the results were coming through on the Tele-printer. We eagerly listened to Dickie Davis reading out the scores as they appeared. "And now the cup soccer."

'I'm glad he got that right," said Andrew.

Douglas chipped in, "Yes, it was a bit of a mouthful." When it came to the Scottish results you could have heard a pin drop as the derby day scores came up.

"Celtic versus Rangers was ... something or other. Dundee one Dundee United . . ." and the screen went blank.

"Oh no!" we shouted. "That's that new slot pay as you go TV run out of money. We will need to get more money from Dad. Whose turn is it this time?"

An hour later, Mum still had not returned, so I went through to the front room to watch for her out of the window and immediately let out a shriek of laughter. The other two quickly joined me and simultaneously laughed out loud.

Hearing all the commotion, Dad quickly appeared to investigate.

The pendulum had melted, and started dripping on to the carpet.

"Right! out the room!" He barked. Then followed us out of the front room and pulled the door firmly shut.

Just at that, the back door opened and Mum shouted through gleefully. "I've managed to get some proper brackets to hang that clock on the wall! We'll get it fixed after tea."

The three of us were trying to stifling our laughter as we followed Dad through to the kitchen to greet Mum.

"Are we getting tea tonight?!" Dad rasped, whilst opening the oven for yet another look at the beef.

"You'll get your tea when it's ready," Mum shouted after Dad, who had already left the kitchen and parked himself on the settee and was settling down to watch Grandstand. "And did you take the lamb out the freezer to defrost?" she asked. "We will eat that tomorrow for lunch."

"Ye-e-sss," he sighed, covertly fetching it from the store room at that moment and placing it atop the boiler to speed up the defrost.

At the dinner table, I commented that the beef was a bit overcooked, to which Dad quipped, "Well, if your mother had been here to see to it."

Mum sharply responded, "The tea was fine until you interfered with it!"

Dad muttered a response under his breath, "Well, you can't see through the glass properly." The three of us just looked at each other.

After tea Mum said, "Right, let's put the clock up with these new brackets I bought."
All the while Dad kept looking silently down at his plate, then announcing he was off to the ice hockey, made a sharp exit.
We all then headed through to the front room led by Mum.
Upon entering, she went absolutely ballistic. "Who did that? No need to ask, I suppose!!........Typical! He's off out and we have to fix his mess! I'll sort him out when he gets back!"

Later, when he returned after the hockey, she said she'd seen his handy work and he replied, "I was only trying to help. If you'd had tea ready I wouldn't have done that."
It had been a long, hard week for Mum and Dad and tempers were beginning to fray. Dad had worked a lot of overtime and managed to find time to cut one lawn, even although Mum had asked him to trim the hedge too, and Mum's spare time had been spent doing several

of her friend's hair for them. which had earned her a few extra bob but had taken up much of her time, so a break was maybe in order.

The schools were off for the autumn holidays the following fortnight and, as Dad was off work as well, and Mum didn't want us all hanging around the house getting under her feet and on her nerves, she had decided that we would all head off to the caravan for a week. "Oh, no!" we all cried on hearing Mum's unilateral executive decision. Dad wanted to say it too, but he felt he best just shut up. We were not excited at the thought of a week at the caravan as all our friends would be at home and there was never very much for us to do, like have a long lie, lounge around watching the TV or mess around in the garden.

"It wasn't our fault Mum, we don't want to go to the caravan!"

This was the caravan that we had pitched in St Andrews where we often went for the weekend and Mum, on the odd occasion, rented it out to help pay the site fees.

"We're going to the caravan, and you'll like it!" she retorted.

"Can Granny Meek come?" asked Andrew

"Well, maybe. We'll see. At least she would help keep her son in check," answered Mum.

On the Sunday evening, everyone packed their things together, ready to set off first thing the next morning.

CHAPTER 2

The next morning, Dad was up with the first sparrow's fart, and had the car packed long before Mum had everything ready, or so he thought.

Mum had been up for hours and had been busy in the kitchen. She was all dressed and ready to go after having prepared the food boxes for the mini holiday. She was now quickly giving the kitchen the once over making sure it was all spick and span in case we were burgled! The dog had already been taken by Mr Crohl from "The Dog Food Shop" for her annual haircut. When she arrived back she immediately ran to hide as she was embarrassed that she looked like a skinned rat. Mum was delighted, commenting on how much cooler Whisky would be. "I didn't realise how fat you were under all that hair," said Mum. "I'll have to get David to give you more exercise when we get there."

The rest of us had been loading the car and bringing everything else, leaving the sink at home and fought for the best seats in the car. A puff of cigarette smoke and the noise of the car back-firing signalled the start of the journey, and the white Hillman Super Minx, with the trendy red stripe along the centre of the side, moved off with its cargo to the caravan. Turning right off the crescent, the car headed down towards the Kingsway as our journey began. Before long, the high observation points of the Tay Road Bridge could be seen.

"Do you remember before the bridge was built, Ron? And the only way to get across to Fife was on the ferry, or The Fifie as it was called. Do you remember what that boat's proper name was?"

"Look, I'm driving! Not playing Mastermind," grumbled Dad. But after thinking about it for a minute he said he thought there had been a few, but the two he remembered were called The Abercraig and The Scotscraig but that there had been others going right back to paddle steamers in the 1800's.

"You could take the car over on them, but we never did. We always got picked up by Eric and Graham's younger brother, Lesley," Mum said.

Crossing the bridge was more fun than usual as Dad maneuvered round the countless cyclists who were paying no attention to the other traffic. Shouts from the back seat of "ten points a cyclist" or "fifty if you knock one over the edge".

Dad, who was a very careful driver shouted back, "Shut up you three. If one of them bangs into me they might get hurt."

Once we had finally made it over the bridge, looking at the way the landscape had been cut away to make way for the road, I commented, "I still think that looks very dangerous, even with the nets."

Mum's monologue had started almost immediately we had left the house, and had only stopped occasionally to give repeated instructions to the driver:

"That's not the way Mr Penny tells me to do it.

"Mr Penny never does it that way!"

Mr Penny was Mum's driving instructor, whose name Dad was, by now, sick of hearing.

"Stop going on about Mr Penny," said Dad. "I need to concentrate. There are blue lights up ahead."

"Where?" said Mum. "I can't see any."

"Just as well I'm driving then, isn't it?" was the reply.

"Can you slow down so we can see what's happening?" came a cry from the back.

'No. We'll just be careful as we drive past."

The blue lights turned out to be someone being breathalysed by the police.

"Try to slow down, Dad," I pleaded. "It looks like a Triumph Spitfire. They're my favorite! And a white one too! Even better. Look at the reg, KFC 1 - Kool for Katz."

Just as we were passing the incident, the policeman was examining the breathalyser and nodded to the driver to give him the all clear. He quickly jumped into the car and moved off gently. No doubt putting the pedal to the metal as soon as he was out of sight of the police which would have set Dad off on another one of his good driving rants. The three of us were like the three monkeys staring out the back window at the police but trying to avoid eye contact just in case we were next to be pulled over.

"Don't you think they should be allowed to have random spot checks?" I asked, to which Dad agreed but said it would hold up honest drivers. "Well, we're OK then, Ronnie," Mum said, "You don't even drink."

"No." laughed Dad, "I can't afford any alcohol, not with all your high-faluting ideas."

"Very funny, Ron," came Mum's response. "Anyway, what do you mean high-faluting ideas?"

"Well, what about that time you advertised your hairdressing salon on Pearl & Dean at the Cinema?" questioned Dad. "Is that not high-faluting?"

"Maybe so, but that paid for the sun porch and you use that, don't you?"

"I use it?" scoffed Dad. "What for?

"To go from the kitchen to the back garden for a smoke."

"Well, there's no beating her then boys, is there?"

"No, but she's got a point." I replied, as usual trying to keep in Mum's good books.

"Well, now that we are in Fife, can we pop in to see my cousin, Graham, and Janet? We drive past Leuchars so it won't be too much of a detour. I thought the boys would like it as they keep chickens now. They even get fresh eggs," said Mum.

Dad grumbled his reluctant agreement through a thick cloud of smoke as he took his last draw out of his cigarette, tossing the butt out the window. "We'll pop in for five minutes, but don't get any ideas that you will be getting chickens and when I say five minutes, I mean five! I know what you and Janet are like when you start blethering and don't think that that means we will be going to see Young Eric on the way home either."

Just then Douglas piped up from the back seat, "Why do you call him Young Eric, Mum, when he is even older than you are?"

"Well," said Mum over Dad's sigh, "his father is Eric as well so he is Auld Eric and his son is Young Eric."

"If Auld Eric's father was an Eric as well, what would he have been known as?" I asked.

"Dad! Smart arse!" said the voice from the haze. "If we went to Eric's you lot would only ask him how he lost the King of Norway's dog."

"It wasn't the King of Norway's dog," stated Mum. "It belonged to one of his entourage."

"Anyway," commented Andrew, "any time we ask him about that, all he ever does is laugh and say 'that flaming dug, I nearly got skinned cos of that'."

The car had now slowed down and fell into line behind a long queue of slow moving traffic until the big yellow tractor causing the tail back reached its destination and turned off into a field. The countryside was now flying past as Dad tried to make up for lost time. Soon the "Welcome to Leuchars" sign appeared on the left hand side of the road and the car made its way to Graham and Janet's house. Graham was my Mum's cousin on her mother's side and was a joiner to trade. A very hard-working and industrious chap was Graham. Mum used to spend her summer holidays at Nanny's sister, Agnes', house, where she got up to all sorts with her cousins Graham, Eric and young Lesley. They would spend their days up Sandford Hill, and Mum being a bit of a tom boy in those days could hold her own amongst her cousins. One year even encouraging them to set fire to the stubble left in the freshly cut fields. Parking outside, we all piled out and filed towards the door. Mum first with Dad trailing on behind her, quickly followed by me and the other two bringing up the rear.

Janet answered the door, smiled with surprise and invited us all in. We were offered the obligatory cup of tea, which Dad, on behalf of us all, politely refused, as he knew if tea came out we would be there for far longer than five minutes.

"We don't really have time as we are headed to the caravan. We just popped in as Margaret wanted to see the chickens."

Pulling a face, Andrew mumbled sarcastically, "Yeah, we all love the caravan, don't we?" As we all made our way out the back to where the chickens were kept, Dad kept slyly checking his watch.

After asking what they ate, how many eggs they laid and all the other interesting questions Mum could think of at the time, she looked pleadingly at Dad. "Can't we just have a few, Ronnie? We can keep them on the grass between the garage and the trees."

Shaking his head, Dad's response was, "And who's going to clean them out then?"

"I can do that!" I said, quickly volunteering for the task. As Dad looked again at his watch, the heavens opened, so he took this opportunity to say goodbye and herded us all out to the car to continue our journey. With the rain lashing down and the window wipers working hard, it was difficult to ascertain which was working more furiously, the rain, the wipers or Mum's jaw. Shortly after, the torrential rain stopped almost as quickly as it had started and the journey continued peacefully with us all taking in the passing scenery, until there was the sharp sound of a gaseous anal emission.

"Cut that out now, the three of you!" Dad roared.

"It was him!" we all said in hysterics.

"Oh, Jeeezus Christ! Who was that?" inquired a booming voice from the front.

"Get the bloody windows open, for heaven's sake!"

It soon became very chilly in the car, so Dad lit another cigarette and soon disappeared into a cloud of smoke once more.

A minute or so later, Mum began to stifle a laugh, much to the disgust of Dad.

"You can cut that sniggering out right now! Did you think that was funny?!" he growled.

"No!" came the high pitched, squealed response.

Dad put the windows back up, then, almost immediately, let out a sudden shout of disgust. "Oh Christ Almighty - was that you?!!" he said, glancing across at Mum, who was now laughing uncontrollably after letting one go as well.

The three of us were in hysterics in the back seat as the smell crept inch by inch throughout the car before almost gassing us.

"Oh miste oh cruddy blighty," I said when the smell reached me.

"Watch your bloody language!" scolded Dad.

"Why? There is nothing wrong with what I said, it was just what you would say but in spoonerism. You know, Dad, when you transpose the first letters of the words." I explained to Dad.

"He's got a bloody answer for everything that one," muttered Dad.

Down came the windows again to get rid of the smell in the car, freezing everyone. Just as we were all beginning to lose the feeling in our fingers from the cold, and Dad was almost ready to put the windows up again, a strange smell began to circulate around the car once more. Everyone was looking suspiciously at each other as we all tried to figure out who was responsible for this particular stench, until we realised it was coming from the herd of cows happily grazing in the adjacent field. "Get those bloody windows up!" screeched Dad.

A short while later, Mum's continuing monologue was interrupted by the sound of a crisp packet being rustled. "Who's eating crisps in the back?! Not in this car you don't! You'll just make a bloody mess!"
We all looked around at the countless empty cigarette packets, sweetie wrappers and old newspapers lying on the floor of the car left by Dad ... which Mum had yet to tidy up.

Finally, we arrived in St Andrews. On seeing sale signs in the passing shop windows we tried to distract Mum but she noticed them anyway and stated, "We must pop back for a look when your gran gets here." At this, we all sighed, as we knew it would mean a day-long traipse around the shop sales when we could be off playing football or walking the dog.

First stop was the traditional visit to the Woollen Mill for a look around, where everyone feigned an interest, before heading upstairs for a free cup of coffee. Opening the door to the large self-service refreshments' room we were immediately hit by the smell of coffee. Seeing how busy it was, and spotting one free table, Mum ordered Douglas to go and sit at the table, quickly, before anyone else got it, while we all filed into the queue so we could make our coffee. Mum announced she had brought some biscuits with her and, surreptitiously, brought them out from her handbag. We all recognised them as the out of date Rich Teas from the back of the biscuit cupboard at home.

Upon dipping a stale biscuit into his cup of coffee, Andrew asked, "How long have you had these?"

"Since I bought them out of Calders!" said Mum

"Oh, yes, Calder's for Aulders!" chirped in Douglas. "How long did they have them for?"

"Stop your moaning, Douglas! I had to sleep in a different bed every night for a year to pay for the caravan," said Mum.

On realising that there was a lull in conversation and everyone else in the room had heard she quickly added, "It's OK. I was being paid for it. It was my job."

"That's enough, Margaret! You're only digging a hole for yourself," said Dad. "These folks don't know that you used to be a carer.

Just then, Andrew gave me a dig in the ribs and nodded towards Dad, who had grabbed the last three Rich Teas and, after dunking them, lowered his head right down and tried to get the drooping biscuits into his mouth. Right at the last minute, he took a final lunge, just as the sodden mush that the biscuits had become, dropped off and splashed into his cup.

Laughing, Andrew said, "Someone pass Dad a teaspoon."

"Not that one, Douglas!" Interrupted Mum. "It looks dirty. Use this spoon, Ron, and when you're done pass me your hankie so I can give this one a wipe."

Dad quickly took the spoon on offer and proceeded to fish out, and consume, the remains of what used to be Rich Teas and then handed Mum the hankie from his pocket.

We always called it the Swiss Army hankie as it was used for absolutely everything, from cleaning the car windscreen to wiping his specs to anything else that needed a quick wipe, but never going anywhere near his nose.

"That's almost as funny as Auntie Hilda when she was here with us," I joked.

"Why?" questioned Mum.

"Well, remember, she got to the bottom of the cafe stairs and pretended to be dying from heat exhaustion, crawling up the stairs and crying feebly out, 'Coffee! Coffee! I need coffee!' After two or three steps, two large Americans appeared at the top landing, stared at the advancing apparition and drawled, 'Well, you're heading in the right direction . . . if you make it!'.

"Sarcastically, Dad had scoffed, 'Well it's free! so Margaret will carry her, if she has to.' At which point the embarrassed Auntie Hilda stood up and marched to the Tea Room. Whilst trying to distract attention from her strange antics, she proceeded to read out all the various names for a toilet which were plastered on the wall, such as 'loo', 'cludgie', 'bog', 'carsie', and many more."

Looking around the table I could see everyone grinning as they cast their minds back to Auntie Hilda's ascent of the stairs.

"Talking about Hilda," said Mum. "We will need to invite everyone round for a meal when we get home. Nanny and Alec and The Menzieshill Mob."

"Is that us then?" questioned Dad. "Let's go. I need a fag."

We all duly followed Dad out to the car, with Mum bringing up the rear, looking for a last minute bargain. All she managed to find was a maroon polo neck for me which was as smooth and comfortable as an auld tattie sack.

As soon as we were out of the shop, Dad lit his cigarette and we all jumped into the car and continued our journey to the caravan. On our first night at the caravan, Dad always went out to collect fish suppers for tea. After waiting for what seemed like ages on him he eventually returned, suppers in hand.

"Best eat them quick," he said "they'll be getting cold by now."

While we all tucked into our semi-warm suppers, I noticed that Dad wasn't eating and, after inquiring what was wrong, Dad with a smug grin on his face said.

"Oh, I ate mine while I was chatting to the man who owns the shop."

CHAPTER 3

The next morning, Dad and we three boys waited at the gates of the caravan park for the bus with Gran on board. When it arrived, a pleasantly plump, small, smiling lady stepped off. Her face broke out into a warm, pleasing smile when she saw the family waiting for her. "Hi, Gran!" We all chorused, followed by Dad's customary grunt of acknowledgment. We all then headed back to the caravan for lunch.

Our caravan was situated on the far edge of the park which gave us, as Gran often said, "a bra view" over the cliffs and the beach. This meant that Mum's ever watchful eye could always oversee us. The caravan itself had two bedrooms, the first of which contained Mum and Dad's double bed and the second had bunk beds where Gran slept when she came. This left the dining-room table and seating area that would be converted into beds for me and my brothers and the dog just slept wherever.

We didn't have all the mod cons in our little caravan, our kitchen comprised of a compact cooker and there was no fridge. This meant that we had to buy food on a daily basis and the milk was stored outside in a bucket of water. There was, however, a small coal fire which was always a good source of entertainment for us boys as we watched Dad trying to light it with the minimum amount of firelighters he possibly could, as he said they were far too expensive to waste. Instead, he opted for screwed up bits of paper to do the job. There was also a small . . . VERY SMALL toilet and, although Mum wasn't keen on the idea, we all used the site toilets which were cleaned daily, as this was preferable to sitting in the caravan after Dad or Douglas had used the loo.

When we all arrived back at the caravan with Gran in tow, Mum greeted her with, "Hi, Gran. You got here safely then?"

"Oh, I thought I was going to miss my bus. I had to wait for the plumber, who did a wee jobby in the bathroom for me," replied Gran, much to the hilarity of the rest of us, with Gran oblivious to why we were all laughing.

As we sat for lunch, Mum announced she had a voucher for a free wine tasting session. This was to celebrate the arrival of the Beaujolais Nouveau, an event where pretentious pseudo-connoisseurs all bestow their opinions upon each other, of "how much better last year's batch was." This was to be followed by a coach tour of Fife, and she suggested we all go that afternoon.

"You'll need to sit up front so you can keep an eye on the driver," Dad mockingly suggested.

To which Andrew asked, "Will we get to taste the wine?"

"Well, you might get a wee taste if you all behave."

"I'm like you, Ronnie. I'm not really a wine drinker," Gran stated, "but I'll enjoy the coach trip."

That afternoon, we all set off to the winery. After an introduction from the guide and a half hour tour of the place, we all headed through to the wine tasting workshop to be given samples of the Beaujolais Nouveau.

Armed with her newly-found knowledge of, and interest in, local wine, Gran nodded in agreement with the guides tasting notes, and (being polite of course) accepted the many offers of further samples, as did her son, the two of them commenting on how each successive sample was better than the previous.

Towards the end of the session, Dad, who was by this point as pished as a proverbial, piped up, "This Boo Jays Noo Velo is very good. I think I'll get a couple of bottles to take back."

He sauntered over to the counter, wallet in hand, but before he bought anything, there came a cry from Mum of, "Ron! Get on the bus now!"

Turning to Gran, Mum muttered, "He'd buy a dead donkey from a door to door salesman if he was told it wouldn't eat much."

Just then, the guide asked if everybody had enjoyed themselves and gave details of how much the various wines cost to purchase.

At this moment, Gran immediately shook her head quickly, put her glass down and exclaimed, "Ach, it's no' that guid, is it?!" before making a sharp exit to the coach to ensure she got a good seat. We were already there, assisting our inebriated father on to the coach. As the coach moved off, Gran peered out the window commenting quietly on everything that she saw and discussing with Mum, Mary Queen of Scots' involvement with Fife, as Mum was somewhat of an expert on Mary through her vast readings of Jean Plaidy novels.

After a while of traveling around Fife, the heat on board was beginning to build on this warm sunny day and the effects of copious amounts of wine were beginning to take their effect on this little, old non-wine drinker as she drifted off into a pleasant snooze.

The tour guide continued to keep most of the passengers totally enthralled and holding on to every word with great interest. Then all of a sudden, out of the blue, came an enormously loud snore which left everybody silent and looking in amusement at the seat where Gran was positioned. The whole bus was silent for a few seconds then the guide continued the interesting narrative. Again, a quiet snore came from the direction of Gran, gradually getting louder and louder, building up in a crescendo and ended by a sharp shove from Mum. The whole time, Dad, who was unsurprisingly not interested in the slightest in what was going on around him, was searching out the window for something to amuse himself with. Getting bored with this almost immediately, he reached for his *Courier* and did his usual paper folding act to ensure it was at a manageable size. The noise he made doing this annoyed the neighbouring passengers, who were struggling to hear the tour guide, and I had to keep ducking to avoid his flailing arms until he cursed, "Bloody paper," and conceding defeat reached for his copy of *The Sun* instead.

Mum looked over and said jokingly, "You'd be better off with my *Woman's Own*," to which Dad, not so politely, ignored whilst he appeared to be looking for a legitimate news item on page three, or any other points of interest.

Later in the afternoon, once we had arrived back at the caravan site, Gran and Mum set to preparing the evening meal and Dad to lighting the coal fire while Andrew and Douglas went out to gather whelks. Me, trying to avoid any trouble that they caused, as with me being the oldest I would get the blame for, decided to take the dog off in the opposite direction for her walk.

In the evening, the three of us were out playing with our football on the site. We weren't gone long when a group of older boys decided it would be fun to bother us, so we returned to the caravan to complain to Dad. Dad, who was busy reading his paper, just muttered something inaudible as he, again, struggled to fold his paper into a readable size. Just then, there was a loud bang as a leather ball bounced off the car bonnet. Dad immediately rose from his chair and marched to the door of the caravan with a stern glower across his face. Upon opening the door, he was faced with the same five, tall, teenage boys lurking outside the caravan, so he quickly pulled the door shut and quietly returned to his seat, peaking every now and then through the net curtains to keep an eye on the trouble-makers who were still hovering about outside.

Shortly afterwards, the apparent trouble-makers dispersed and so we went back out to play. However, we weren't out long before a girning Douglas returned hastily to the caravan once more, complaining that the troublesome older boys had hit him on the head with their leather ball.

At this, Dad became enraged. "Right. That's it!" He exclaimed, before storming to the door of the caravan, shouting and with fearsome gesticulation of his arms at the young lads causing the trouble outside. Soon enough they ran off, not to bother us again! Dad returned to the caravan, face red with anger. He lit a cigarette then assumed his previous position on the couch, picking up the newspaper to continue reading.

At the end of the night, as we were preparing to go to bed, Gran came bursting into the caravan and in a loud voice exclaimed.

'That's an utter disgrace!!"

'What is?" inquired Mum.

'Those toilets! They're an utter disgrace! I've never seen toilets as utterly disgraceful as that! There's no lock on the door! No toilet seat and the bowl is disgusting! It's an utter disgrace."

'Whereabouts is this Gran?" questioned Mum.

"Just up at the block, the toilets! Come and see it," complained Gran, as she led Mum out of the caravan and marched her off towards the toilet like a small Sergeant Major with a vengeance, still muttering, "Utter disgrace," under her breath as she went.

A few minutes later they returned to the caravan, Mum in hysterics.

"What was it Mum?" we asked.

"Well, Gran's dead right! She would have fallen down that toilet if she'd used it, with one leg trying to keep the door closed, because she wasn't in a toilet, she was in the slops room for throwing out the waste."

Everyone looked at Gran and laughed, but none laughed as loudly as Gran herself.

The next day, Andrew and Douglas headed out after breakfast to play, while I went down to the beach with one of their spades. All the rainwater which had drained off the fields, had channeled into a pipe which emptied on to the beach where it collected into a large, damp patch on the sand. I spent the next few hours using the edge of my spade to create a shallow, wiggly channel in the sand, which directed the water any way I wanted on its way back to the sea. The shallow channel quickly became deeper and wider and I was soon having great fun building dams to create pools and redirecting small channels anywhere I wanted. Master of the water, I was enjoying the peace and quiet away from my brothers for a short while.

Gran and Mum headed down to the town for a look around the charity shops. After a while, Gran and Mum returned, Gran displaying her lovely new 'fan' coat which she had bought in one of the charity shops, after Mum had haggled with the sales assistant to get the price down. We later discovered that 'fan' was nothing to do with the shape, but rather Dundonian pronunciation of the word fawn.

Mum took out from her bag, the brand new nylon bed-sheets that she had bought in the sales to show us and bright red pyjamas she thought would do Andrew. The sheets are easily washed, quick to dry and they don't need ironed she informed us. "I must look for more when we get home to Dundee," she said.

"Yeah, look for some more for yourself, Mum," muttered Douglas under his breath, as if to say...and see how you like them. Douglas and I immediately christened Andrew cherry blossom due to the colour of his new pyjamas.

'Oh!" cried Mum, "You should have seen this shop. It was amazing! It sold everything you could imagine. It was like the one on that TV comedy. What was it called, Ron?" After waiting for Dad's response, to no avail, Mum continued with her story, "I couldn't tear your Gran away from the underwear department when she saw they sold six packs of gent's underpants. She thought a couple of packs would do well for Bill and Dad's Christmas. Your Dad could certainly do with them as those old cotton ones he wears end up looking like he's wearing a nappy."

"What? Like a sumo wrestler?" asked Gran.

"No. More like Ghandi," Gran had seemingly spent a good ten minutes inspecting the pants, rubbing her fingers up and down the spaver bit, she had apparently been very bemused and had wondered how men do the toilet through this strange gap.

"Oh, and we also got some flip flops for you boys. They are very handy for on the beach and it will stop all that sand ending up in the caravan," continued Mum.

"Did you have flip flops when you were young?" Andrew asked a very disinterested Dad.

"No," came his response, "we were bottle fed." He said with a raised eyebrow. He then proceeded to milk as much laughter as possible from his little joke as he looked from one of us to the other, squeezing out as much accolade as he could from this one liner, until

Mum's staring face crossed paths with his gaze like a sledgehammer, and all signs of merriment were immediately wiped from his face. Deciding it would be best to try and get back into Mum's good books he went into the bathroom to clean his teeth.

All of a sudden, all the power in the caravan cut out, and a gruff voice from the dark declared, "Jeeesus Christ! Is that you overloading the electric again?! Too much on at one time trips the switch and who's been squeezing the toothpaste from the middle again? I can't see a bloody thing in here. Oh, Christ all bloody mighty! The tube's burst and it's squirted out the side all over me!" raged Dad.

As Dad emerged from the bathroom, we all tried to hold in the laughter as no one wanted to be the one to tell him that the toothpaste had squirted all over his jersey.

"Right! You'll need to go up and get the key to switch it back on again…and you can pay for it this time!" moaned Dad.

Gran and Mum got in the car to go and pick up the key but were gone a lot longer than Dad expected.

Upon their return, Dad asked, "Where have you been? That took ages. I had to wash the toothpaste off my jumper myself in the dark."

"Well, we nipped in to town to get a couple of copies of the key cut. It will save all the hassle next time the power cuts off! As long as they don't find out."

"And money," Dad muttered under his breath.

As we were sitting down to lunch, there was a heavy knock on the door. Opening the door, Mum was faced with a large, ruddy-faced farmer with enormous hands that were all gnarled and calloused from years of honest hard work, who was ranting and raving about two of her sons stealing his turnips.

"Well, it would not have been my children. They are well brought up and wouldn't be doing anything like that." said Mum, offended at the suggestion.

"It was definitely your boys. Eh ken whit they look like! There's that curly haired ane and thon ane wi' the blond hair," raged the farmer, who seemed to be getting redder by the minute.

At this, Mum shook her head and informed the farmer politely, "Sorry, but you must have the wrong boys."

While they were arguing as to whether it was or wasn't her boys who were to blame, there was a shout from some distance behind the farmer.

"Mum! Look what we've got for the soup. We got some to take home for Nanny and the rest too!"

She peered round his large frame, while he turned also, to be greeted by the sight of Andrew and Douglas pushing a shopping trolley full of turnips. Black affronted Mum apologised to the red-faced farmer in front of her and assured him that she would deal with them appropriately later. But first, she insisted that Andrew and Douglas took their plundered neeps straight back to the farm, with the farmer accompanying the neep nickers to make sure they did and didn't just dump them halfway there.

Being the oldest, I would usually have got the blame when my two younger brothers got up to mischief . . . (as I was supposed to know better) but this time had avoided the turnip hunt to take the dog for a walk on the beach. Serves them right, I thought when I returned later to hear of their antics.

That night after dinner, Mum and Gran set about changing our bedding to the new, nylon sheets they had bought that afternoon. As it was late and were all quite tired anyway, we all went to bed soon after, ready for an early start the next day.

Next morning, Gran and Dad were up first, as usual. The noise of them banging about wakened up Mum and the three us and we then got up, immediately, after having an uncomfortable, sweaty night. Dad mentioned that the three of us were up earlier than usual and Mum asked how the new sheets were.

"Mum, I hardly slept all night because I was sweating and I still feel wet," I replied.

"Same here," agreed Andrew. And Douglas said he had just slithered about all night and complained about still feeling hot, sweaty and sticky. Mum reckoned we must have had too many sheets on but when we asked how she managed, she said that they could only afford them for us and that they had had to use the cotton ones, so we were to think ourselves lucky. So they had obviously had a more comfortable night than us.

The final couple of days passed quickly as the time for us to return home loomed ever closer. Our last few days were spent exploring our surroundings with the eagerness of children.

On one of the evenings, Mum and Gran decided it would be fun to take us all over to the big house on the site for the evening's entertainment, as Gran had heard at the toilet block earlier that there was to be bingo, a band and a buffet and IT WAS ALL FREE!!. This house was a former stately home which stood at the centre of the park, surrounded by neat, never ending rows of uniformly placed caravans, which differed only in the size of the door mat. The house, which was once a grand mansion owned by Lord somebody or another, was now used as the entertainment hub for the caravaners. In it there was a bar and restaurant which we never usually got to go to as Dad said it was far too expensive. There was a chip shop and fast food takeaway downstairs and round the back, which we never got to go to as MUM said it was too expensive. On the other side of the ground floor, there was a small newsagents that sold all our favourite comics, sweets and funny postcards which, we never got to go to as GRAN said it was too expensive and, working for D.C. Thomson's, Dad would sometimes get "free samples" of comics anyway. The final part of the ground floor was used as an arcade and was full of slot and gaming machines, which we never got to go to because we had no money anyway and we'd already spent the money Nanny had generously given us on the quiet. Up the stairs was the grand ballroom in which the night's entertainment was to take place.

"Get a table near a window, away from the bar, Ron," said Gran, "and not to close to the band either. I can't be doing with all that racket when I'm trying to talk."

Dad looked at us, winked and said with a laugh, "Get a table near the band boys."

"You'll do no such thing," said Mum, "There's one free over there, close to the buffet. That will be perfect."

"Too late," laughed Andrew. "Gran's already got it." We all settled into our seats, while Mum checked in her bag to see what biscuits she had left to keep us going till the buffet was served. Andrew volunteered to go up to collect the bingo cards and was taking quite some time, while he chatted to the young, attractive girl who was handing them out. He came back just in time for us to hear "eyes down for the top line".

"What does that mean?" asked Mum, who claimed she'd never played bingo before in her life.

Dad grimaced while he explained to Mum what she had to do.

"2 and 7, 27," started the caller.

"Got it!" said Mum, as she ticked it off her card.

"No. 2 and 7 is 9," argued Gran.

Again, Dad explained.

"Well, what am I crossing off?" asked Mum, "27 or 9? I've got both."

"Just the 27," said Dad with a sigh, who was now beginning to get slightly irritated.

So Mum, making sure she'd crossed off 27, accompanied it with, "Definitely got it."

Looking up at Mum, the caller announced, "On its own, number 9."

To which came the response, "Got it."

A couple of "got its" down the line, with the caller looking at Mum and shaking his head with every one, Mum said, "I don't know what he's shaking his head at me for, I've no numbers left on the top line anyway."

Just at that "house" was called on the next number. "You should have shouted house when you'd filled your line, Margaret," said Dad, frustrated.

"I didn't know that. Did you know that, Gran?" asked Mum.

"Know what?" questioned Gran. "I've not been paying attention, I've been watching Andrew with that young girl across there."

The game continued with the caller shouting for a full house and Dad, again, having to explain what this meant whilst Mum complained to the caller that she couldn't remember the numbers that had come before. The caller who was now trying his best to ignore our whole table, left the explanation up to Dad, who was by now wishing he was at the ice hockey and wondering who was daftest, his Mum or his wife or possibly himself for agreeing to this trip in the first place.

The game continued without too much more interference from Mum, with the whole room concentrating in silence, until Douglas who was by now bored, stood up, and with a mischievous grin pointed to the corner shouting, "MOUSE!" To which everyone, thinking he'd shouted "HOUSE", started the usual moaning and grumbling about how they only had one number left to get. Pretending to be apologetic, Douglas walked away smiling saying, "Sorry. I thought I saw a mouse."

"I told you, Margaret," exclaimed Gran, "you'll need to get that laddie looked at. There's something no' right wi' him."

Gran won the full house bingo and was horrified to find that, after all that effort and confusion, her prize was a ceramic goat, which looked as if it was smiling at her. Slightly embarrassed, and more than a little disappointed with the grinning beast, she went up and collected it from the caller. Returning to the table Gran asked, "What am I supposed to do with that ugly thing? It's certainly not going on my mantelpiece."

"Just leave it on the chair when we go," said Mum.

"No, they know which door mat's ours. They'll find me. I'll wrap it up and give it to my brother Bert for his Christmas."

After filling ourselves full on the buffet, we watched Mum entertain the room with her solo Shake and Vac dance. Mum then went over to the compere and requested some Scottish country dance tunes for 'The Pullars from Dundee'. A group of American tourists were first to reach the dance floor and did a pretty poor attempt at The Gay Gordons, followed by an even more peculiar version of The Dashing White Sergeant, which everyone in the room was finding very amusing. As the spectacle unfolded in front of us, I laughed and said . . "If we laugh at them too, people will think they're the Pullars, instead of us."

When the music started, Mum went over to Dad and they started dancing together. Dad soon got bored though and so did his Zebedee act. "Time for bed!" We were all ushered out and soon back to the warmth of the nylon.

On the day before we were due to go home Mum decided to get a head start on the packing while Dad took Gran to the bus station. She would have to get the bus home as there wasn't much room in the back of the car and, with the three of us, it was a tight enough squeeze as it was. "I need to get home sharp anyway," said Gran, "I will need to be on the ball tomorrow as Mrs Grimmond has a week off and I'll have to do all the work."

"Can't you just give her a cough sweetie?" sniggered Andrew. At which point he headed off to the rocks in search of whelks with Douglas, and to distance myself from their antics, I headed off to the beach with the dog, hoping the exercise would help her loose a bit of the excess belly weight she was carrying. Arriving at the beach, we went straight down to the water. I had decided that a bit of swimming might be a good source of exercise for her. Knowing that Whisky wasn't keen on swimming, I put her in to the sea and she quickly swam out. As soon as she shook herself dry, I picked her up and threw her back in. I thought to myself, this will soon slim her down. Again, she immediately swam straight back to shore. As I bent down to pick her up and throw her back in, she looked at me as if to say, "Please don't do this to me again."

Feeling sorry for her, I gave her a reprieve, thinking to myself, "I've tried my best. She will just have to stay fat." Noticing this sign of weakness on my part, she took the opportunity to run hell for leather all the way back to the caravan, with me in hot pursuit to make sure she didn't get lost.

Arriving back at the caravan I was relieved to find Whisky already there, but not so to see Andrew and Douglas returning arguing over who had collected the most whelks.

Mum told them that Gran had said it would be best to leave them steeping overnight in a bucket on the floor and they would be able to take them home when we left the next day. "Will Whisky not drink the water?" asked Andrew.

To which Mum replied. "I wouldn't think so. It will be salty from the whelks."

'I'm not keen on seafood. I think it's the salt water that puts me off anything in a shell, what do you think Mum?" I asked.

"I like shellfish. I've tried most types. I've never had crabs though," came the reply, followed by our stifled laughter. "That's enough from you three," scolded Mum. "Time for bed."

So the bucket of whelks was left to steep in the middle of the floor while we all headed off to bed.

The early morning peace of the next day was shattered by Dad's moans of, "Oh! For god's sake! What's happened here?"

This brought us all rushing from our beds to find the bucket of whelks had been knocked over in the night by the dog and they had crawled all over the caravan in search of water.

So, before we were fed, we had to play hunt the whelk with Douglas asking, "How many were there?" and Mum trying to mop up what was left of the water.

After all the whelks had been hunted down and breakfast had been consumed, we all piled into the car for the drive home. With Mum saying "Well, we've all had a good time. Ronnie, try to cut down on the smoking on the way home."

"I will only smoke them one at a time, Margaret." said Dad, sarcastically.

CHAPTER 4

We arrived home that afternoon and all filed into the house one by one.

Mum commented, "What a horrible stench! What is that? Is it the dog?"

"No. The dog's not in yet!" shouted Andrew.

We all agreed that there was, indeed, a weird and nasty smell but no one seemed to be able to find the source.

Mum spent the rest of the afternoon preparing a chicken with all the trimming for tea, so that we were all fed and ready for the arrival of "The Menzieshill Mob" that evening.

As Mum sat down to tea after serving up the rest of us first, I said, "This chicken tastes a bit funny."

"There's nothing wrong with it!" she replied curtly. "Just eat it!"

"It tastes kind of sweet. Are you sure it isn't off?" I moaned.

"Well, mine is perfect!" said Mum and Dad in surprising unison.

"I'm sure there's something wrong with it. It must be off." I repeated.

"I've forgotten my juice, I'll just go through and get it," Mum informed us all, like it was something we all needed to know.

"Where is it?!" was the cry from the kitchen. "Has someone thrown it out?!"

"Oh no. There it is," she said as she picked it up to take a drink.

"Eww, no! This is the gravy! I must have put the orange juice in with the chicken instead of the gravy!"

"That'll be the chicken that there's nothing wrong with...?" I remarked

Mum just laughed it off and sat down to carry on with her tea. As soon as everyone had finished, Mum set about tidying up and doing the dishes, while Dad read the paper, which meant we got the pick of what to watch on TV.

Meanwhile, up in Menzieshill, Bill, Hilda and Alison were all waiting for the taxi to arrive to bring them over to us for our weekly games night, which this week was to be Trivial Pursuit. As soon as Alison saw the taxi coming up the brae, she nipped over for Gran, who lived across the road. Gran came out the door sporting her new 'fan' coat, her green hat and her usual broad smile.

The guests arrived in their taxi at 7pm on the dot. First through the door came Auntie Hilda followed by the jovial faced, happy-go-lucky Bill, then Gran and, lastly, the teenage Alison with her short, thick, dark brown hair.

"Hi Hilda, how are you doing?" greeted Mum.

"Oh, not too bad, Margaret. I'm just always so tired these days. It's terrible!"

"Hmm, have you been to the Doctors? Maybe an idea if you're always so lethargic."

"No, no, I'm just tired, that's all. What's that horrible smell, Margaret?"

"Oh, we don't know Hilda. It's worse in the kitchen, come through and see for yourself. It smells a bit like Bill when he's had corned beef for his tea, don't you think?"

Just then Granny Meek followed in and repeated, "Oh, that is horrible! Smells like Bill after he's had a bowl of my Scotch broth."

"Oi! That's my husband you're both talking about!" cried Hilda. "You could be right though, although it smells more like he's been at the Vindaloo."

"We've got a man coming round to service the boiler next week. Do you think it will have cleared up by then?" said Mum hopefully.

"It's a nice night, Auntie Margaret," observed Alison. "So while they set up the game, I could do your highlights in the garden." Alison was interested in hairdressing and, later, when she left school had worked in a salon as an apprentice for a while. As Douglas and Alison were the same age and, at this point in their lives, close to the same build, Mum once got Douglas to try on a dress that she had bought Alison for a gift. We have always thought this was very funny. He was very cute . . . 'nice face, shame about the legs'.

"Good idea. We'll do it on the patio." And out they went, Alison carrying the equipment and Mum carrying a stool.

Alison teased Mum's hair through the skull cap and added the highlighting fluid.

As she was working away on Mum's hair, they were interrupted by the screams of the next door neighbour, Martha, "...I don't know, I'm not Superman! I cannae see through windaes!" Alison and Mum just looked at each other in surprise, shrugged their shoulders and continued with the job in hand.

"I'll go and check if we're ready for the game yet, just sit here in the sun till I come back for you," said Alison.

As she went in through the kitchen she saw Gran preparing cups of tea, so helped out with that, and took it through.

We all had a cup of tea and a piece of cake, tidied the plates away then sat down to play the game.

"Where's your mother now?!" snarled Dad.

Suddenly Alison remembered. "Oh no! I've left her outside!" and rushed off through to the patio to get Mum.

"Sorry. I forgot you, Auntie Margaret. I was helping Gran. Oh, I think I've maybe left you a bit too long in the sun."

"I'm sure it will be fine," was the reassuring reply.

They both headed in through the house to the front room, to be greeted with shrieks of laughter, as everyone saw the streaks were more like peroxide bleach marks rather than highlights.

"I'm awfy sorry, Auntie Margaret," said Alison. "It must have been a combination of the sunlight and the length of time."

"Oh, it looks quite nice, actually," Mum said. "Do you want to try Uncle Ron's now?" To which Dad gave it the response he thought it deserved . . .

As we all settled down to play the game, Mum inquired, "What's hat on your knee, Hilda? It looks nasty."

"Oh, it's my psoriasis."

Dad teasingly offered, "Well, if you got off it occasionally it might not be so sore!"

"No, Ronnie, it's not that. It's a skin complaint." Mum said sharply as she handed round the box of remaining After Eights from the previous week and everyone hastily ate as much as they could before the next person grabbed the box. When it finally reached Dad, he made three unsuccessful attempts at selecting a mint, each time only managing to grasp an empty packet, punctuated with the usual, "Jesus Christ". After this third unlucky attempt, and with his frustration growing, Mum begin to snigger, and was at once shot down with a, "Shurrup Margaret!!!!"

Mum forced herself to stop, instead, holding it in with a cheesy grin.

"Oh, cut it out!" snapped Dad. "I want to show Bill the video player before we start playing the game."

"Is that the new video player you were telling me about, Ron? I've never seen one before, but my cousin Brian has one. You know Brian? Brian who plays for St James with us," said Bill excitedly, going over for a closer look.

"Yes," replied Dad chuffed that Bill seemed impressed, "It can even record programs when you're out." "How does it know when you're out?" inquired Granny Meek.

Dad staring at her intently responded sarcastically, "Probably because the house is quiet."

Just at that, the film that had been showing ended with the MGM Lion's trademark roar and Mum and Auntie Hilda shouted, "There's Ronnie!" and explained for the hundredth time that this had been what they used to say in the cinema.

Everybody settled down and Bill said, "Right, let's start the game."

"Margaret, what is the capital city of France?"

"Let me think...

"...of France?

"...capital city?

"What was the question again...?"

"What's the capital city of France?" Bill repeated.

"Oh! I know. Paris! We've been there. Do you remember that, Gran?"

"Talking about going places," said Mum. "Ronnie has just sent away for his new passport, the form asked if he had any distinguishing features and he's got a beauty spot just near that freckle."

'Where?" questioned Auntie Hilda, "that's not a beauty spot, that's a wart!"

Gran, as usual, immediately jumped to Dad's defense commenting on what a lovely-shaped head he had, with Uncle Bill adding that he looked like Yule Brynner with that hairstyle. Gran, again, defending

Dad, said it was his lovely, big, almond-shaped eyes and thin lips that gave him the look of Yule.

"Can we get on with the quiz?!" said an exasperated Dad, while looking at his watch.

"It's your question, Mum."

"Right. Gran, what has a maiden filly never done?" asked Bill in a suggestive tone, whilst trying to stifle a laugh.

"...Oh, I, I don't know," said Gran sheepishly.

"Well, think then. Just make a guess," piped up Douglas.

"OK then. Is it, had sex?"

"No!! You dirty old wuman! That's just filth! Why do you always bring it down to that level," shouted Bill, jokingly, bringing the question card down with a joking blow to her head.

"Oh!" exclaimed Mum. "That reminds me, we watched that program Your Life In Our Hands last night. It was all about a sex change operation. There was this woman on that was becoming a man."

"That would gee me the wullies," said Gran.

Sniggering Douglas replied, "Well that's the point, is it not?"

Bill hastily changed the subject and continued playing the quiz master, some questions being answered correctly, some wrongly, but everyone argued and discussed each answer at great length.

Then it was back to Gran's next question.

"Right Gran", said Bill. "What is a man suffering from if he has diphallic terata?"

"Oh! What's that then?" Gran enquired.

To which Bill responded, "Well, that's the question, you daft old bugger. Here, look for yourself."

"Don't really know. Will I turn over and look at the answer?" asked Gran.

Two penises was the answer. But Gran mistakenly read this out as "two pennies".

"Talking about that," piped up Alison. "In English class today the teacher told us that his niece had asked him what a penis was. He said he had thought about it carefully and was about to answer her, but before he could get it out (at which point the entire class erupted in laughter as he went red with embarrassment as he realised what it sounded like . . . his niece said 'don't be daft, it's a man that plays the piano'."

Hilda then gave Alison a stern look and shook her head.

'Oh, I've had enough of this." mumbled Douglas "these questions are all about sex. If it's not about a man with two willies we're talking about some woman getting one. I'm away to run up to that new Indian takeaway next to Gibson's. Anyone want anything?" asked Douglas. With no response from anyone he waltzed off shouting over his shoulder as he left, "Well, don't think you'll be getting any of mine." The front door closed then immediately reopened as he came back in announcing that he had just come back for a jacket. Running upstairs, he shouted on his way out again, "Definitely no one wants anything?"

On further thought I decided to go with Douglas. "Ach well, I might have something. I'll come with you and see what they have. At least they don't sell sweet and sour chicken like we had for tea." Putting my jacket on, I left with Douglas.

Looking up, Douglas said, "It's looking very dark, we'd better move."

Walking up the crescent, Martha and Bob arrived back from their weekly big shop. Martha and Boab, as she called him, lived with their three children nearby. Martha was Arbroath born and bred, with the thick accent to prove it. A kinder and more generous person, anyone would be hard pushed to meet. On seeing them Douglas called over, "You better hurry and get that shopping in. It looks like there's going to be rain soon."

"Oh, I didn't realise it had got this dark. Boab, hurry up and get those bags in," replied Martha.

"Right enough. She cannae see through windaes," I said to Douglas and we both set off again up the road laughing away to ourselves. Further up the road, we could see Campbell just going in his front gate.

"Hi Cammy," shouted Douglas. "We're going up to the Indian for a takeaway. You coming?"

Looking up at the sky Campbell responded with, "I've had my tea, but I'll come with you anyway." Campbell was at the same school as us, and a cannier more pleasant mannered guy didn't exist, he truly belied his thick, curly, red hair.

Continuing on our journey to the takeaway, we could see Brian Davidson at his front door with his golf clubs. "You off golfing Brian?" I asked.

"No, I'm just back. I was out earlier with my dad."

"We're nipping up to try that new takeaway place," said Douglas.

"Oh right, we had one from there last night. It was really good," replied Brian. "See you on the bus Monday, Dave."

The further up the crescent we walked, the colder we felt and the cosier each house began to look with the warm glow coming from behind their curtains.

Trudging on, Douglas and Cammy were busy chatting and I was now slightly in front of them, calling out I shouted, "Come on you two, get a move on before the wind gets up, it's cold enough as it is." At this they both began an exaggerated quick march and, arms swinging about like clockwork soldiers, soon they had overtaken me. "Who's holding us up now?" was the sarcastic comment from Douglas. Catching up with them we pressed on, they tired of their childish nonsense and with the hilarity over we soon made it to the warmth of the Indian, even the smell of the hot spices seemed to warm us up.

As we looked through the menu, trying to decide what to have was proving difficult as none of us had tried Indian food before. Cammy and Douglas decided to look for a recommendation from the woman serving behind the counter by asking what each item was and constantly changing their minds as each new dish was described. I was becoming put off the thought of buying something as the woman Douglas was talking to had one tobacco stained tooth in her top jaw and what looked like only one chipped tobacco stained tooth in her bottom jaw. We had been told that she had been a looker in her day but that must have been many years ago. After eventually deciding what to have and placing our order, we enjoyed the warmth and the smells of the shop until our names were called and our food was ready.

Just as we were about to leave, Douglas asked the woman "Do you have chicken breasts?" When she nodded yes, Douglas replied, "Oh, that's good, but I'll stick to my pakoras for now, fluffy tits!" as he edged towards the door announcing quite loudly and for all to hear, "Well, back into the breach lads, that's my cockles well and truly warmed now!"

Stepping out of the shop there was a flash of lightning followed by an almighty crash of thunder and the heavens opened. Pulling on his hood and running for home whilst trying to keep the food dry, Douglas said, "Bet you wish you'd brought a coat now, Cammy?"

Cammy, whose bright orange, curly hair was by now a sodden, soaking mess replied, "Yeah, but I'm almost home, you two still have a bit to go."

We kept running until we reached Campbell's house and he took off up the path, calling out as he disappeared in the front door, "See you later, lads."

We carried on running down the road and in the back door into the kitchen, throwing off our wet coats we placed the takeaway on a tray, grabbed a few tissues for napkins and a couple of forks and made our way through to the front room.

On seeing us Mum said, "Oh, you didn't get caught in that rain, did you?"

"Nah, it's just sweat, Mum," was my response, "and there's still a smell in the kitchen, by the way."

"We'll just sit here with our stuff. You lot carry on, although I thought you'd be finished by now," moaned Douglas.

"That food smells really nice though," said Alison.

"Well, you were offered," replied Douglas

"Oooh! And it looks like there's lots as well," observed Hilda.

Douglas, picking up one of his pakoras, asked me how mine were.

"Really nice," I said, "worth getting wet for."

Looking around the room we could see the longing looks following our every mouthful. "I think I've got too much. I wonder if Whisky would like one? Seems a shame to waste them, especially since they smell so good."

Eventually, giving in to the puppy dog stares Douglas said to Alison. "You'd bring a tear to a glass eye. Have one of these."

Pretending not to care too much, Alison replied, "Only if you're sure you have too many. I'll try one."

Dipping one in the sauce, she ate it in a oner. "That's really nice," she said. "What's it called? Oooh! It's really hot!"

"Pakora," said Douglas.

"What are they?" asked Hilda.

"Just cow's testicles with a spicy sauce," sniggered Douglas.

At this Alison gagged and ran full pelt through to the bathroom.

When she came back, she indignantly scolded Douglas with, "Cows don't have those anyway. Which reminds me, I'm throwing out some of my old dresses, do you want a look through to see if you want any?" she said, hoping to bring him down a peg or two.

"That's enough you two," said Hilda.

"I'm sure there's a want about that laddie," said Gran. "Are we playing this game?"

Just as we were about to start the quiz again Uncle Bill, the quizmaster, piped up. "Wait till I tell you about the football training. We were all in the shower after the match and one of the guys said he had found a lump down below. When he went to get it examined the doctor looked at it from every angle, gently feeling the lump between his finger and thumb. The doctor had then quickly squeezed it and it went 'pffsssssssst', everyone in the shower grimaced. I thought Wullie Karl was going to pass out at the thought. Turns out it was nothing to worry about - it was just a fatty deposit."

Looking round the living-room, Bill could see that everyone here, including the women, were grimacing at the thought of it too.

"Did you have that last pakora, Alison?" asked Dad, laughing.

"I'll just nip to the loo before we get going again," said Bill.

Knowing that the toilet was a dangerous place to go after Bill had been, everyone rushed to try to get there before him. As soon as everyone was out the loo, the fight for the comfiest seat began. Everyone trying to secure a place on the gold, brushed velvet three piecer so that they didn't have to sit on the floor. Douglas and Alison had to sit on the foot stools with Gran in between Bill and Hilda and the rest of us all squeezed in somewhere, bringing in stools from the other rooms. I tried to get a space near to Bill so I could possibly get a sneaky look over his shoulder at the answers. Just as we had all got comfy and Bill was about to start the next question, the evening news was just finishing with a story about Tutankhamen. Andrew looked up and remarked how he had been told about that at school just before the holidays. Apparently archaeologists had opened up a

Pharaoh's coffin from a pyramid and were painstakingly trying to unwrap the mummified body to see how it had been preserved.

Douglas watching this said bemusedly, "Well, I can't see him surviving."

Bill who had noticed Dad beginning to get impatient, was trying to continue with the questions, noticing too Auntie Hilda added. "Alison it's your turn, are you playing or watching TV?!"

As usual, sticking up for Alison, Gran exclaimed, "But it's Top of the Pops on now Hilda. Look, it's Johnny Mathis. I like him!"

"He's a poof" laughed Alison.

To which everyone looked at her horrified, as none of us had really used this word in family circles before.

Bill, looking around for something else to eat, broke the silence, with, "Here's your question, Margaret. "What is 15 in Binary?"

"Oh, you'll know that, Hilda," said Mum. "You were in the binary department, weren't you?"

"No, I was in the Binding department," replied Hilda.

Bill, the question master, then had a question for Gran. "Here you are, Gran, here's another one for you. It's right up your street, too!

"What is a castrated Bulls known as?"

"Ah... well... in Scotland it's stots."

Bill corrected, "No. Bullocks."

"No, it's right," Gran argued, innocently. "Talking about that, I saw Mrs Grimmond the other day. Remember I work with her. She said her daughter is getting married to a farmer's son. It's to be in St James Church in the Ferry, that one you used to play football for, Bill."

"Thank you for another piece of useless information Gran." laughed Alison.

"Did you enjoy your pakora, Alison?" laughed Douglas.

"Your mother said that's enough!" growled Dad.

A short time later . . . after the game had come to an end and realising it was getting late, Hilda said, "Right Ron, we probably better be heading. Will you take us up the road, please?"

"Oh Bill, before you go, my Mum, Nanny, has made an extra fruit loaf for you to take home with you cause she knows you like them," said Mum.

"Ooh, that's good. I'll just eat this last slice before I go. It looks lonely and no point in wasting it. Thank her for me the next time you see her, will you."

"I'll do that, she's coming out tomorrow afternoon."

And with that they all headed out the door to the car. Bill with the fruit loaf in hand and the evening was over.

CHAPTER 5

Around lunch time the following day, we heard the distinctive clip clop of Nanny's heels coming round the path. The dog, Whisky, knew what this sound meant and ran about really expectantly and when Nanny came in, laden with goodies, the dog leaped up on her hind legs to try to get up to Nanny as she always did.

After saying hello to everybody, Nanny put down her bag and took off her coat. She was a tall, slim, bespectacled lady, who immediately set to work making scones and pancakes, which were something legendary amongst the family.

Alec, Nanny's husband, was coming out later. Alec was a few years younger than Nanny and they met in the Nethergate Bar where Nanny worked as a waitress and he worked part-time as a barman. Over time they had struck up a friendship, as they were both now on their own due to Nanny being widowed just after the war and Alec being a divorcee. We always thought that he resembled Jim Bowen from Bullseye - tall, bespectacled and a very similar face. He had gone into the town to pay the rent, then was heading over to his friend's house to speak to him about getting our gas fitted up again Alec worked for the Gas Board, in charge of the stores, and you didn't get anything from his store room unless you had an authorisation chitty signed in blood, in triplicate. He didn't care who signed it as long as it was signed and his books balanced. Indeed, at his retiral, many years later, the younger colleagues had said that they would have given him a bottle of Whisky but they didn't have the proper authorisation. The previous week, Alec had been in Perth with this friend for a Gas Board Convention, regarding the reconstruction of the verification and authorisation protocol and procedures manual, or as Alec called it, "how to make sure no one gets bugger all".

After a long and tiring day, trying to look like he was paying attention to all this superfluous information that he would pay no attention to anyway, Alec and his friend had decided to nip into the nearest pub "The Half a Sixpence" which was owned by Mum's cousin, Ray, for a couple of pints.

A few pints and a couple of nips later!!! Alec had left his friend, who was to be staying in Perth anyway, and headed off in the direction of the train station, stopping in at the nearest R.S. McColls for a newspaper and some mints.

Getting on the train, the first compartment he came upon had a family with noisy kids. Avoiding this one and the next one, which was no smoking, he moved along the train looking for a suitable place to sit. The third compartment he found was empty. This is where he made himself comfortable. Taking his jacket off and laying his fags, sweets and paper out on the table, he slumped down into the chair with a sigh to enjoy the temporary rest. Taking advantage of the peace and quiet, Alec relaxed and took in the view. As the train passed across the rail bridge he wondered what on earth those daft buggers were doing out on the island at this time of night! Were they playing golf or had they just escaped from Perth Prison?

The train moved on slowly, gathering speed, with Alec watching the moon bouncing off the waves in the Tay. The noise of the wheels trundling round and round and round and the hypnotic glow of the moon along with the trees going past faster and faster and faster was too much for the fortified Alec and he drifted off into a sound sleep. The warmth of the carriage keeping him comfortably oblivious to the fact that the train had now passed through Dundee and was now heading off up the East Coast link to Aberdeen.

The next thing Alec was aware of was the clatter of people getting on and off the train, and the station's P.A system announcing where the next stop would be. On hearing the announcement and realising that he had missed his stop, Alec quickly jumped into action grabbing his jacket, fags and mints and headed swiftly towards the door leaving his paper behind on the table. Realising it was late, Alec looked at his watch to see if he could make the last bus back to Dundee. Seeing how late it was, and knowing that the buses would now be off, Alec had had to phone his friend, Jack Hill, that worked with him part-time in the Nethergate Bar to come through from Dundee to pick him up. So we were all hoping that he would make it up from the town this time without any mishaps.

"Oh, how did last night, go by the way?" enquired Nanny.

Mum responded, "Really well. We had a right laugh. That Trivial Pursuit you brought back from Canada is a great game and your baking went down well, too. Bill thanks you for his fruit loaf."

Just then, I walked in the back door, informing Mum and Nanny that a coal lorry had spilled its load on the Kingsway, just at the bottom of the road.

"You should see it! Half the road's shut off 'cause of all the coal. I was lucky to make it home. That's the start of rush hour, it's getting pretty busy so there's loads of traffic. I was going to stop and see if I could help but, I promised I'd come home early to help Dad change his flat tyre so you can get your car back."

On hearing about the coal lorry, Mum and Nanny looked at each other and immediately took off out the back door to get the barrow from the back garden. We all knew they were heading off to try and get some of the spilled coal. Just like they had done a few years back when a lorry-load of potatoes had overturned on the Kingsway.

She shouted through to Dad to come out and help as well, but he responded, "No. I'll have to stay here and help David with this tyre of mine."

So off went Mum and Nanny down to the Kingsway to pick up as much coal as they could carry in the barrow…and do their bit for road safety!

Douglas and I headed out to the car to deal with the tyre. "So much for Dad coming to help!" grunted Douglas. "Oh! He must be on his way out, I can smell the fag smoke!"

A minute later Dad appeared, fag in mouth, to offer his expertise.

Douglas was hunched down trying to take the plastic hub cap off to get at the wheel nuts, and was pushed aside by Dad who said, "I'll do this bit," as he fitted the wheel brace to the plastic nuts on the hubcap.

"No. You've got to…" Douglas tried to protest, but was interrupted by a sharp crack as the plastic nut snapped off.

At this, Dad laid down the wheel brace and made an abrupt retreat to the house, making his excuses to go and "check the oven", leaving Douglas and I to carry on changing the wheel.

Just at that, the boys heard the out-of-tune whistling trademark of a happy, cheery man coming along the avenue.

"Whit ya daein', lads?"

"Just changing the wheel, Alec. Could you go and get the other foot pump from the garage?"

"Aye, nae bother. Back in a second. I'll just go and pop these things in the hoose that your mum asked me to pick up for her."

A short time later, Mum and Nanny returned, wheelbarrow laden with coal. "There's a tonne of the stuff down there!" said Nanny. 'And that's a fact!

'There was some funny, wee man come roond tae see yae, Margaret. He said he was fae the kirk."

"You never did a very gaid job o' gettting the fat aff that dug," joked Alec. "I just seen her and she looks fatter than ever."

"Oh, that would have been who the boys call The Penguin. Thank goodness I was out. I'm far too busy to blether with him today," answered Mum.

The Penguin, as we called him, was an elder from the church. He always wore a black suit and stood with his hands clasped behind his back and his feet splayed outwards, giving him the look of a penguin. He was a very nice, but uninteresting, man who seemed only to nod and say "aha", "mmm", "ah". Unfortunately for me, he was the uncle of a school friend which meant if he came to the house when Mum wasn't in, the others left me to talk to him.

"What about that other lady from the church. The one that works in the bank. She's a nice woman. Has she found herself a man and got married yet?" asked Nanny.

"No," said Mum. "I think she's too wrapped up in her work and having a good time with her friends, although she won't die wondering, if you know what I mean!"

"Oh well, that's good, because she's no spring onion."

"I think you mean chicken, Mum."

"Yeah. That's what I said, Margaret," agreed Nanny.

Leaving us to wonder exactly what she meant, Mum headed off round the back with her barrow full of ill-gotten gains.

"Oh, hi Alec," said Nanny "I didn't realise you were here. Did you pick up my prescription when you were in the town?"

"What prescription? You never said anything to me about a prescription!"

"Oh, I must have forgotten. Well, maybe you can pop in town again tomorrow and collect it for me?"

"Och! You'll hae me swearin', Jean!" replied Alec.

Hearing Alec's voice, chef Ronnie appeared from the kitchen after adjusting the temperature of the oven. "Oh Alec, glad you're out. Got a wasps byke in the shed. I could do with your help getting rid of it."

"Nae time like the present, Ron. If we get crackin', we can get it done afore yer tea's ready."

Dad and Alec headed off towards the shed, deciding on the way, that they would try and smoke the wasps out. Finding an old bucket, they started a small fire with a few old, oily rags, and stood back and watched as the dense smoke began to fill the shed. As a few wasps started to appear Dad and Alec, armed with a frying pan and a tennis racket, began whacking as many of the escaping insects as they could. At the time neither of them could see the cruelty in this and were like two school boys having fun as they picked them off one after another, staring adversity square in the face without flinching just like a couple of musketeers . . . or so they thought.

When I smelled the smoke, I went outside to see what was happening. Horrified at what was going on, I explained to them both that I had been learning about this in school and the teacher had said if they left the wasps with the smoke they will go away on their own.

"Is there nothing they don't teach you at that school?" moaned Dad.

"Well, if there is, they've not told me," came my smart-mouthed reply.

"I'm getting bored of this anyway," said Dad. "It must be about time for a cuppy. I'm away in to see if they have the kettle on."

"Yes, let's go and leave them alone. They won't do us any harm anyway," I said heading off in the direction of the house. Just as I was about to go into the house an enraged wasp deciding to take its revenge and not realising I was on their side, aimed its stinger and took a runny at me, or should I say a buzzy at me, and ferociously stung me on the bum!

Dad, in his usual concerned manner said, "Did they not teach you that at school?"

We all wandered back into the house to hear Andrew replacing the phone receiver, with his usual, "Thanks for calling". A technique he regularly employed to disguise the fact he was responsible for the majority of the monthly phone bill!

"I don't see very much money in that phone call jar!" observed Mum.

"Ah, that was Harry phoning me!" replied Andrew.

Mum invited Nanny and Alec to stay for tea, much to the disgust of Dad, as he knew he would be on taxi duty at the end of the night.

We all sat round the table, at the usual time of 5 o'clock, as Mum prepared to serve up the tea with the help of Nanny. Dad told Andrew, "You better go and get a cushion off the settee for your brother, he might think you're a pain in the arse, but he's got one all of his own tonight."

As Mum went to take the roast chicken out the oven, she announced innocently, "Oh, look Ronnie! It's come out smaller than when you put it in, and it's all shriveled up! That always disappoints me a wee bit."

We all smirked at each other stifling a laugh, with Mum apparently oblivious to her double entendre, and Nanny afraid to comment.

We all sat round the table in the dining-room, Nanny still busy, apparently, pottering about in the kitchen.

Dad reached for the salt cellar almost robotically and tipped most of the contents over his food.

"Are you coming through to eat your tea before it goes cold, Nanny?"

"I'll be through in a second. I'm just stuffing tomorrow's turkey!"

A moment or two later, Nanny wandered through to the dining-room with a puzzled expression on her face. "What part of the turkey does this belong Margaret?" laughed Nanny, suggestively, holding the neck of the turkey.

"You know very well that's the neck, Mum, and have you remembered to take the gubbins out? Not like Martha next door."

I think the word she was looking for is entrails not gubbins.

Meanwhile, Douglas made a sly remark about the flat tyre, to which I sharply responded to my younger sibling, "Are you taking the p…."

"Peas and carrots anyone?" interrupted Nanny, "And Douglas, be careful with those mashed potatoes. Don't drop them in your drink like Bessie at Christmas."

"I've not been drinking," moaned Douglas.

"Oh, I remember that Christmas. That was the year Bessie got a little bit tipsy and accidentally dropped some mashed potato in her glass but she was enjoying her drink so much that she downed it in a oner saying 'I've got tattie wine'," laughed Alec

Bessie was married to Will, who was Nanny's brother. To us, he looked like the fat one out of Laurel and Hardy, with his big, bald head, enormous waistline and, like all the males on Nanny's side of the family, stood over six feet tall, with his garth, as he called it, holding up his trousers well over his belly. Will had never truly grown up as he was full of fun and still up to as much mischief as he could get away with at his age. (The oldest scallywag in town.) Bessie was his perfect match, his soulmate. You could tell by looking at her that she enjoyed a wee drink now and again. She echoed his size but not his height and she couldn't pronounce her 'L's properly, so to our endless amusement always called him Wuway. This provided us with a continual source of entertainment as we tried to imitate her.

"Anyway, I don't have a drink yet," chimed in Douglas.

'Well, don't think you're getting wine. There's Ribena under the sink. Go and help yourself. You can see I'm busy," replied Mum.

Heading off to the kitchen to get some, Douglas shouted through, 'This isn't Ribena. It's Blacord. That's a cheaper version."

Mum, who was beginning to get annoyed at him replied, "It's exactly the same stuff. The only difference is one of them has got no added additives and the other one hasn't."

"That was braw soup, Margaret," Alec said.

To which Mum replied. "Yeah, Ronnie likes me to give him a ham shank in the soup. It all adds to the flavour."

As we all sat enjoying dinner and conversing, Nanny inquired about the previous weekend at the caravan.

"Oh, it was a good laugh," said Mum.

"Dad really enjoyed it," I added, sarcastically.

"On with your tea," was the blunt response from Dad.

"How did Granny Meek and her brother, what's his name, Bert, isn't it, get on when they had their weekend away?" inquired Nanny, trying to change the conversation somewhat.

"Oh, she said they really enjoyed it, but Bert let himself down as usual. They had to sleep in the same room and Bill, Alison and Hilda shared the other one.

"Why? What did he do?"

"Well, the first night he got up 3 or 4 times for the toilet which kept waking Gran up, so she suggested he used a bucket. Which he did."

"But one night, she woke up to the noise of Bert weeing in the bucket and then as he stumbled around trying to find his way back to his bed in the dark, he lost his balance and knocked the bucket and it went all over Gran! When she asked him why he hadn't switched on the light, he told her he hadn't wanted to waken her!"

"Oh, really," said Nanny. "I almost feel like I was there!"

"I wish you were," Dad mumbled under his breath.

"I hear Bert's moving round the corner to The Glens," said Nanny.

"Yes, you were offered a perfectly good house round there a few years back but you turned it down. I still think you should have taken it. You'd have been better off there than where you are now and Bert would have been a pal for Alec," replied Mum.

As we finished off our meal, Dad, who was finished first as usual after only eating half of the plateful, sat back in his chair. "Well, if that's my tea, I've had it!" said Dad. Like he did after every meal, never realising the hard work and effort Mum had gone to.

"So, what's for pudding?" was his next comment.

"Stewed balloons and custard," sighed Mum. That was Mum's polite way of saying, 'whatever you get you won't be happy with anyway'. We all knew that it meant we would not be getting anything we loved such as Instant Whip, jelly and ice cream or, the best of all,

Nannies steamed pudding. It was more likely to be sago, tapioca or, as Dad so eloquently called it, sema-bloody-lina.

Alec piped up, "Oh, I really enjoyed that, it was good hen, thanks!"

"I take that from my Gran, Granny Goodie, with her huge family she had to improvise and could make a meal out of nothing, given the right ingredients."

Later in the evening, as Dad was grudgingly getting ready to take Nanny and Alec home, he remembered, almost gleefully, "Oh, the buses are off next week cause of the strikes, so you might not manage out!"

"Oh don't worry, I'll maybe just walk it." answered Nanny.

Dad, looking disappointed at this, wondered to himself why he was required to give a lift at all.

"Right! Your chauffeur awaits. And you lot make sure you leave some of those pancakes and scones for me when I come back."

And off they headed, amidst choruses of "Cheerio Nanny!".

CHAPTER 6

A couple of days later, we were awaiting the arrival of the maintenance man to service the boiler. He arrived early, just after 9am and carried his tools through to the kitchen with the assistance of Douglas, before getting to work.

"What the fffflaming heck is this?!" shrieked the boiler man, working alone in the kitchen, as he discovered a packet of rotten lamb atop the boiler. "How long has this been here?" He questioned Mum as she ran into the kitchen to see what all the hullabaloo was about.

Looking embarrassed at the sight of the rotten meat Mum said, "Oh my goodness! I've been wondering where that awful smell was coming from. That must have been there since before we went away to the caravan.

"Ronnie, was that you that put that there to defrost?" she asked the cloud of smoke as it disappeared out the back door.

Once he had finished servicing the boiler and was packing up his tools, Mum, still feeling slightly embarrassed about the lamb but grateful that he had uncovered the source of the smell, offered him a cup of tea and one of Nanny's scones, which he enjoyed.

Just then Dad, walking in, moaned quietly to Mum, "What are you giving him one of those scones for? There's hardly any left!"

"Well, he's done a good job, AND he discovered what that smell is! I don't suppose you know anything about lamb on top of the boiler or do you?!"

The following Thursday, despite the most atrocious conditions of the year, with torrential rain coming down, Nanny duly appeared just after lunch. Her arrival signaled as usual, with the familiar clip clop of her heels on the back path and the dog going frantic. She was laden with gifts from Markies for us and had walked all the way from Charleston in the torrential rain due to the bus drivers being out on strike.

"I'm here, Margaret. I just walked, that's the worst rain I think I've ever seen. And that's a fact."

"Oh, very good, now how the heck are you going to get home?" muttered Dad.

After taking off her coat and setting down her bags, Nanny asked the familiar question of, "Right, Margaret. What are you needing done? How about the ironing?"

"Yeah, that would be a great help, Mum, then if you, like I'll do your hair."

Later on, once the housework was all done, Nanny said to Mum, "If you could give my hair a tidy up, Margaret, that would be fine."

So Mum washed and set Nanny's hair in the kitchen. Then took her out to the shed with a magazine and a cup of tea, with the wee, fat roly poly dog waddling behind. "You can keep me company, Whisky," said Nanny.

"I'll pop back in the house and get you a biscuit to have with your tea. I think I have some shortbread left, but it might be a bit soft, so I'll stick it in the oven for a couple of minutes. That's what Granny Goody used to do."

Mum returned to the make shift hair salon with her freshly-heated shortbread.

"There you go, Mum, just like new. I'll come back out for you once I think your hair's dry and, after we've had tea, Ronnie will give you a run home."

"Oh, that's good. I've brought a rhubarb tart that I baked this morning. It's in my bag. I've also brought another fruit loaf for Bill as I know he loves them and really appreciates it. After all I was baking anyway so a fruit loaf doesn't take much more effort and that's a fact."

A short while later the rain had gone off and Mum returned to check on Nanny's progress. "That's you all dry Mum, you head in and I'll switch things off here."

"Well, check and see if the dog's still in there, I didn't see her leave," shouted Nanny over her shoulder as she headed off towards the back door.

Bending down to switch off the drier, Mum discovered Whisky huddled in the corner on a pile of old rags. Trying to usher the dog out the door Mum realised the reason for her explainable weight gain over the past few months. She had just given birth to three puppies and she was using the pile of old rags as a nest for them. Rushing excitedly back into the house Mum announced, "You'll never guess what's just happened? Whisky's had three puppies."

"No, she's not!" exclaimed Nanny, "I'd have noticed that! For goodness sake, Margaret, there's nothing wrong with my eyesight."

"Well, come on and I'll show you," said Mum as she marched off towards the shed again with Nanny and the rest of us all in tow. pointing at the puppies she said, "Three puppies, Mum . . . and that dear Mother, IS A FACT."

Lying on the rags in front of us lay Whisky and three identical miniature Whiskys.

After we had all had our turn for a look, Mum decided we should all go back to the house and leave the dog in peace to take care of her litter. She told Douglas to go next door to get Diane as she thought she would probably like to see the puppies.

Diane, hearing the news of our new arrivals, came round immediately. She and her parents, Stan and Winnie (or as we called her Flossy) had lived next door for a few years and also had a Westie called Rough. Diane was the same age as myself and was a tall girl with very long, light brown hair. Her ambition when she left school was to become a midwife, so it was a shame she had missed the actual birth. Looking in astonishment at the puppies with Diane, Mum wondered who the father might be as Whisky never really came into contact with other dogs. As if reading Mum's mind, Diane volunteered.

"I know who the father is! It was Rough what done it, I saw them."

"Did you not stop them?" questioned Mum.

"Well, obviously not!" I said pointing at the evidence.

"What are we going to feed them?" asked Douglas, as being the youngest he didn't realise that for the next few weeks Whisky would take care of that herself. Although she didn't seem very maternal at the time, but this was most likely because she was very young herself.

"Since it was Rough what done it, does that mean we get one?" asked Diane eagerly.

"We'll keep a white one for you." I replied sarcastically.

After we had all had a good look at the puppies we said goodbye to the Lawsons and headed back into the house for tea with Diane calling after us, "Remember one of them is mine."

While we were having tea Dad asked Nanny when she thought Alec would next be round as he needed to speak to him about a tree.

"Is that the rogue tree at the back bedroom window?" asked Nanny.

"What's a rogue tree, Nanny?" asked Douglas

Nanny's explanation was that a rogue tree was a tree grown from a seed dropped by a bird.

"What do you mean?" questioned Douglas "Out its mouth?"

"No! Out its arse! In its droppings!" mumbled Dad.

"Anyway, I need to talk to Alec about getting it cut down as it's getting too tall to be that close to the house and it wasn't a rogue tree as you call it. That's the sapling I dug up when we were out for our Sunday drive in the country."

Mum reminded Dad that she had told him at the time that the tree would grow far too big where he had planted it.

"It doesn't matter. I'll talk to him about it when I drop you off. If you're ready, and we go now, I'll get back in time for the ice hockey."

So Nanny said her cheerios and clip clopped of down the path towards the car.

CHAPTER 7

The end of the Autumn holidays was drawing near and soon we would all be back at school, so Mum had decided that as it was the last weekend before school started it would be nice to have everyone round for tea. By everyone, she meant Nanny and Alec and all The Menzieshill Mob.

Mum busied herself all morning tidying the house and preparing the food for the meal later that day, as usual, her progress was hindered by Andrew and Douglas squabbling and messing around.

"Can you all just get out from under my feet and let me get on. They'll all be here before I'm ready if I don't get a move on," shouted Mum in exasperation.

"Well, if you let us go up to the Swannie Ponds we'd be out of your way," suggested Andrew.

The Swannie Ponds, or to give them their correct name "Stobsmuir Ponds" or Stobbie Ponds, were home to the resident swans which was where their local name came from. There were two ponds, the bigger of which had an island in the middle and this was where they had the dinghy's that you could hire and paddle about until you time was up. The second, smaller pond, was where people used to sail their small remote control boats and fish for sticklebacks with nets on the end of a long cane. There was also a putting green and grassy areas. In all the years we used to go to Swannie Ponds as kids I only ever saw a swan once, although everyone else used to see them all the time.

After giving this suggestion some thought, Mum decided that they could go if, and only if, I went with them as we were all in our good clothes ready for the visitors and she knew I would try and keep them out of trouble, and only if we were home before five. Not overly enthusiastic at this idea, I decided to round them up and head off out, just to get them out of Mum's way.

As we headed out the front gate Avril, from down the road, who was out in her garden shouted hello and waved to Andrew.

"There's your lass waving at you Andrew," I laughed.

"She's not my lass!" came his reply

"Well, what were the two of you up to in the bushes at the side of the ice rink not so long ago then?" butted in Douglas.

"We were only looking for empty lemonade bottles so we could collect the thrupence at the V.G," he answered, his face getting redder by the second. Trying to change the subject, Andrew said that we had best get moving or it would be time for us to head home. In agreement, we all headed off up the crescent.

Passing Martha's house, Douglas inquired with a smirk on his face as to whether Andrew and Lynn McEwan had spent any time recently looking for empty lemonade bottles. Ignoring this comment, Andrew walked off in front. Our first stop along the way was at Gibsons at Douglas's request as he wanted to buy some sweets with the money Nanny had given us last week. Douglas and Andrew spent what seemed like an eternity looking at the penny tray and the tuppenny tray trying to decide how they could get the most amount of sweets for their money. Both decided not to spend everything but to keep some back for later and, on leaving the shop, immediately started to stuff their faces whilst we headed off in the direction of the ponds.

Going along Clepington Road we stopped at the Coke-a-Cola factory to stare through the window at the bottles on the conveyer belt. One by one the bottles were filled and then sealed closed by the sea closing thing fixing the caps to the bottles. All amazing technology to us. Even although it was a Sunday, there was still one man working and when he saw us looking in he came out with three bottles of Coke. On handing us each a bottle he said, "Dinnae tell naebody, lads."

Straight away Andrew and Douglas headed to the nearest fence post to see if they could prize the caps from their bottles, whilst at the same time moaning to each other that the man could have opened them for them. After a few minutes trying they managed to open their bottles by using the edge of the post and proceeded to devour the Coke. Wanting to safe mine for later, I stuffed mine into my trouser pocket and shoved my hanky in on top to stop it falling out. Ushering them along, I reminded them that time was passing and we hadn't even arrived at the ponds yet. We all hurried along the last, short distance and finally arriving at our destination we argued about who was first and what was the best dinghy. Once we had all decided on what dinghy we were using we started paddling round and around the island. We seemed to spend forever going round and around and around the island, really exciting or so we thought? This continued until, for some unknown reason or just out of pure mischievousness, Douglas decided he would try to get on to the island. Paddling up to the edge he managed to grab hold of the brickwork that surrounded the island and pulled himself as close as he could. With the dinghy touching the edge and Douglas with a tight grip on the bricks (white knuckles and squeaky bum) he leaned forward and tried to stand up, at which point the dinghy slowly began to float backwards. The dinghy ever so slowly moved further and further away from the island and as Douglas was STILL holding on. He began to get lower and lower, and closer and closer to the water. Andrew and I would have rushed to his assistance had our laughter not taken over but, as it turned out, we didn't have time anyway. By now he was fully outstretched and just inches from the water, muscles straining and with sinues almost tearing, discovering he couldn't beat the laws of physics or Newtons Laws of Gravity he finally succumbed and slipped face first into the pond. The creature from the Swannie Lagoon rose from the dark, murky depths . . . of the four inches of water and walked indignantly back to shore through the many cat calls of "No Paddling" along with Andrew's comment of "especially with your best clothes on."

As Douglas emerged from the pond, I told him he should have been more careful. My friend, Hedgie, did exactly the same thing when we went there with him and Steve last year. I decided we had better head home quickly as Douglas would now have to get changed before the family arrived. Andrew and I started to run down the road with Douglas squelching, dripping and shivering along behind us

We headed off towards home and, as we approached the shops, Douglas asked Andrew to go in to buy him some more sweets with his left over money since he was traumatised from his near drowning and needed to keep his blood sugars up. To which Andrew agreed on the condition that he got some of the sweets, meaning he could keep his own money for tomorrow. I over-ruled this plan, because we needed to get home quickly. We were in enough trouble already because of Douglas and if we arrived home late I would be the one to get the blame.

Running down the road Campbell was, as usual, messing about in his front garden, we shouted "Hi Cammy, can't stop we're late!" and continued on our way.

Arriving home, Douglas tried to sneak in and change before being spotted and I went into the kitchen to open my bottle of coke which promptly exploded and sprayed everywhere due to it being in my pocket as we ran home. This, unfortunately, did not amuse Mum (no sense of humour that one), but it did divert her attention from Douglas, who she noticed trying to sneak upstairs, and he got off scot free.

"For goodness sake, David. I asked you to take your brothers out of my way so I could get on and now, thanks to you, I've got Douglas and the kitchen to tidy up again. Get out from under my feet and go up to the Nicol and Smiberts van for me and get some of their cheap, leftover cakes," moaned Mum.

"If Nanny's coming, will she not bring some homemade stuff with her?" I asked.

"Don't answer back, David. Just get on with it, I've got enough to do as it is now without your smart remarks and you can wipe that grin off or you'll be laughing on the other side of your face in a minute."

"What's going on in here?" asked Andrew.

"And take him with you as well," called Mum after me.

Shortly after Andrew and I arrived back with the 'leavies', the rest of the family started to arrive. Luckily, Mum had miraculously managed to get everything tidied up and back in order before they got there. Nanny and Alec arrived first, followed closely behind by The Menzieshill Mob in their taxi. Coming into the living-room Granny Meek was saying hello to everyone whilst having a good old moan about the taxi driver.

"That blooming taxi driver, his driving was terrible, the speed he was going at you would think he was driving in the Grand Prix.

was bouncing about all over the place. I think I've got a concussion and, to top it all off, the door shut on my shoe."

Miss-hearing this Dad said, "Well, I hope you wiped your feet properly on the way in then if you've got dog shit on your shoe."

After everyone's laughter had subsided Dad, fed up with being the butt of the joke, slumped wearily down into his chair with a long, loud, lingering sigh.

"Can we stick the TV on for a minute so I can catch the football results?" asked Bill.

'Well, it's a new TV. It got delivered earlier today, so I hope you've got some change in your pocket for the meter," said Dad jokingly. 'It's one of those new-fangled TV's from Telebank. You put money in the meter and you can watch it for a couple of hours. That way I don't get an enormous bill at the end of the month, it's all paid for up front. If there's more money than needed in the meter to pay the rent at the end of the month I get that back, so it's like save-as-you-go as well as pay-as-you-go," boasted Dad.

What Dad hadn't told any of us was that it was our first colour television. You could either watch it in mono or adjust the settings and it watch in colour. When Andrew turned the television on it was set to mono, so it came on with the usual black and white picture.

Dad asked Andrew to adjust the contrast using the middle button and, not knowing this was really the colour button, he did as he was asked and the set burst into colour. The first time any of us had seen a colour TV. This was Dad's sense of humour. He gleaned pleasure from the surprised looks on everyone's faces and, as none of us except him had know that it was a colour television, he got the reaction he was after.

Meanwhile, Douglas who had managed to sneak in the shower without Mum noticing him had reappeared in the living-room wearing fresh clothes.

"Why have you changed? What happened to your smart, good clothes you had on earlier? You know I wanted you to wear them today. And why have you got that jersey on? You know it's different colours." said Mum agitatedly.

Douglas had come downstairs wearing a green pullover that used to be mine until I wore through the elbow. Nanny was going to darn it but decided she would be quicker to rattle it down and redo the whole arm. Unfortunately, when she did, she had used a slightly different shade of green which, due to her bad eyesight, she hadn' noticed but it meant the jumper had one arm which didn't match.

I had noticed this at the time but was, as usual, over ruled by Mum. It was a different story now though.

"It doesn't matter. Everyone is here now and we're about to eat soon, so you don't have time to change. Come and say hello to everyone."

"Oh, that reminds me," said Nanny on seeing Douglas. "Can I have a rake through your button box while I'm here, Margaret? I need two buttons for Alec's gardening shirt and I don't have any that fit in my box. It's an old shirt so I'm not buying new buttons for it."

Mum and Nanny both always cut the buttons from our old clothes before they threw them out and kept them in a box - just in case.

"I've heard of everything now," laughed Hilda. "Keeping the buttons from old clothes. That takes the biscuit. But while you've got it out, can I have a look for one for Bill's work trousers."

"Me, too," joined in Alison. "It's the school disco next month and the blouse I want to wear is missing one."

After they had all finished their button hunt, Mum said, "Teas ready. Everyone through to the dining-room."

Groaning as he wearily rose from his seat and turning off the TV to save money, Dad ushered everyone through.

As we all sat around the table enjoying our food, Granny Meek asked Nanny how she was getting on with the young couple that had just moved in upstairs.

"Oh, they're very nice, but the boyfriend has had to move back to his mum's house so that the young girl doesn't lose out on her benefits."

"You'd think she'd get more benefit if he stayed," chuckled Bill quietly.

"I heard that! That's enough of that, Bill," replied Hilda.

With that the conversation died down as everyone continued to eat, until Alison piped up . . .

"Why do we call you Granny Meek, Granny Meek when Uncle Ron's name is Pullar and so was Mum's before she married Dad?"

"Meek was Granda Sam's name, who I married many years after my first husband, Dave, died. He was your Mum and Uncle Ron's dad and his name was Pullar. He was killed in the war whilst on special operations which were quite secret so no-one knows exactly how he died. That is who your cousin David is named after as his name was David too," explained Granny Meek.

Chipping in Mum added, "David's middle name is James, after my father."

"So who's Auntie Marion then?" asked Alison.

The rest of us knew that Auntie Marion was Granda Sam's daughter from his first marriage and we all listened as Granny Meek explained this quickly to Alison.

"Did your Mum not do something important in the war as well, Nanny?" asked Douglas.

"No, that was my Gran, my Granny was a F.A.N.Y."

"A what?" laughed Andrew.

Uncle Bill was about to reply but the look on Auntie Hilda's face told him not to bother.

After all the childish laughter had subsided Nanny indignantly explained to everyone that F.A.N.Y. stood for First Aid Nursing Yeomanry, a very important group of female volunteers.

"I'll bet," agreed Bill.

"Was that Granny Goodie?" questioned Douglas.

"No. Granny Goodie "Goodfellow" was my mum, not my gran."

Granny Goodie was indeed Nanny's mum. She had had ten children, including Nanny, who was the oldest and the youngest was her brother, Joe, who was just slightly older than our Mum.

"Another one who didn't die wondering," said Bill quietly, nodding to Dad.

"Now that we've had 'This is your Life' can we get on with tea. What's for pudding, Margaret?" came Dad's usual war cry.

"Just jelly, fruit and ice cream," said Mum.

As everyone began to tuck into their overflowing pudding bowls, a strange noise was heard in the room. Everyone immediately looked at Bill

"Why are you all looking at me like that?" asked Bill.

"Well, the strange noises usually come from your direction," laughed Hilda.

"Well, that one wasn't me!" said Bill, pretending to be offended at the very suggestion. "That was Gran with her jelly," at which point we all joined in trying to make our jellies do the same.

After we had all finished eating and trying to make the flatulence noises with the jelly, we headed back through to the living-room where the adults were going to have coffee. There was the usual mad scramble to get the best seat. Dad didn't have to take part in this scramble as no-one dared take his.

As Dad came into the living-room his face changed when he saw Granny Meek perched quite happily in his chair and, without saying a word, he silently sat elsewhere as his Mum was the only person that could get away with this.

"That's a braw heat coming aff that fire now, Ron," said Alec.

"Yes. And the best part is that the coal's all free. That's still the stuff we salvaged form the overturned lorry last week," chimed in Mum, chuffed at the thought of a wee saving.

Andrew then told everyone the story of how, around a week or so ago, Dad had just backed up the fire with coal to last the whole evening when the phone rang. It was Nanny who had phoned to say that her brother, Dite (Dave), was up from Manchester and was staying at the Angus Hotel. Dite had a successful business down in Manchester and was pretty well off, and had booked the best suite in the hotel so he could have a family party while he was here. All the Dundee relatives were invited and some staff from the hotel would be going too. As soon as Dad heard this he instructed us all to get our coats on while he spent the next ten minutes on his hands and knees carefully taking off as much of the coal as he could, safely, from the freshly-stocked fire so as not to waste it.

"Yes, well, your mother had paid for THAT coal," said Dad.

Mum, who had gone back through to the kitchen to finishing making the coffee, shouted through that there didn't seem to be any electric working in the there.

"Bill, you're an electrician. Go and check the fuse box for her," said Hilda.

"I know what to do," I said. "I'll go and do that."

As Bill was enjoying the heat from the fire, he gave me a thumbs up and nodded so I headed off to the fuse cupboard.

On reaching the cupboard, I opened the fuse box and found the offending fuse. As I tripped the switch Mum shouted through that everything was working fine again. Proud of myself on this great accomplishment I sauntered back through to the living-room, "Well, that's that sorted. What else can I do around here that I'm dead good at," I announced as I turned on the big light.

Flicking the switch to turn on the light, there was a sharp crack and the whole house was plunged into silent darkness. After a few seconds of silence, everyone spontaneously erupted into loud cheers and the sound of laughter and clapping filled the room.

"Any candles anywhere?"

EPILOGUE

Those days are gone now and so has my hair and Douglas'. Dad has more hair than both of us put together, albeit mostly up his nose, a possible glimpse as to what the future may hold for us (like father like sons?). Andrew, for some reason has managed to keep his hair (he always was a stingy bugger). Mum is still smiling and in charge, looking after us all. In the following years, I went on to become a Quantity Surveyor, Andrew became a successful DJ and worked his way up through the ranks in BT with Douglas following Dad into DC Thomson. We all eventually settled down and had families of our own, which meant Mum and Dad were Grandparents to Stephen, Barrie and Lisa and Louise and Jennifer.

Over the years, as with every family, we've had our arguments and our falling outs but certain events throughout our lives have taught us that family is everything and we are all still here together, stronger than ever.

FAMILIA PRIMUM

copyright 2017 by David Pullar

Printed in Great Britain
by Amazon

71795430R00066